A **TRUE** BOOK™

The New Hampshire Colony

KEVIN CUNNINGHAM

Children's Press®
An Imprint of Scholastic Inc.
New York Toronto London Auckland Sydney
Mexico City New Delhi Hong Kong
Danbury, Connecticut

Content Consultant
Jeffrey Kaja, PhD
Associate Professor of History
California State University, Northridge

Library of Congress Cataloging-in-Publication Data

Cunningham, Kevin, 1966–
    The New Hampshire Colony/Kevin Cunningham.
        p. cm.—(A true book)
    Includes bibliographical references and index.
    ISBN-13: 978-0-531-25392-2 (lib. bdg.)   ISBN-13: 978-0-531-26605-2 (pbk.)
    ISBN-10: 0-531-25392-9 (lib. bdg.)   ISBN-10: 0-531-26605-2 (pbk.)
    1. New Hampshire—History—Colonial period, ca. 1600–1775—Juvenile literature. I. Title. II. Series.
    F37.C86 2011
    974.2'02—dc22   2011007144

All rights reserved. Published in 2012 by Children's Press, an imprint of Scholastic Inc.
Printed in China 62
SCHOLASTIC, CHILDREN'S PRESS, A TRUE BOOK, and associated logos are trademarks and/or registered trademarks of Scholastic Inc.
1 2 3 4 5 6 7 8 9 10 R 21 20 19 18 17 16 15 14 13 12

Find the Truth!

Everything you are about to read is true *except* for one of the sentences on this page.

Which one is **TRUE**?

T or F   New Hampshire Colony was begun by people wanting freedom to practice their religion.

T or F   The Stamp Act was very unpopular.

Find the answers in this book.

3

Contents

A colonial blacksmith

New Hampshire general John Stark

THE **BIG** TRUTH!

New Hampshire's Founding Fathers

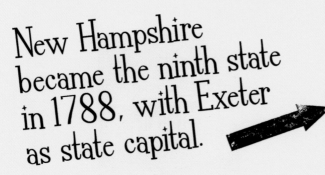

New Hampshire became the ninth state in 1788, with Exeter as state capital.

Timeline of New Hampshire Colony History

1500s

Abenaki dominate the area.

1603

Pring explores Piscataqua River.

1623

The New Hampshire Colony is founded.

1774

Patriots raid Fort William and Mary.

1788

New Hampshire becomes a state.

CHAPTER 1

The Real People

Early Native American peoples came to New Hampshire at least 10,000 years before Europeans came to colonize it. Several groups speaking related languages dominated the region by the 1500s. These included the Pennacook, Winnipesaukee, and Ossipee peoples. The area groups together became known as the Abenaki. *Abenaki* was a native word meaning "real people."

Food From the Wild

The various Abenaki tribes had their own customs. But they shared many everyday habits. They built no permanent towns. They instead moved from place to place and set up winter and summer villages. They often returned to the same general areas. The Abenaki made hunting a central part of life. Abenaki men used bows and arrows or short wooden spears to bring down deer and moose.

A hunter prepares to bring down a moose from his canoe.

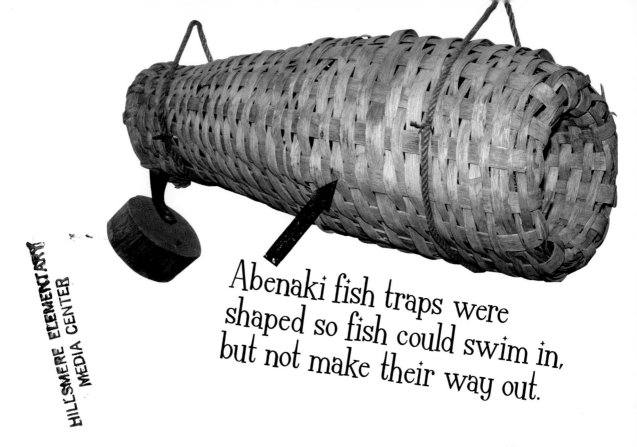

Abenaki fish traps were shaped so fish could swim in, but not make their way out.

The Abenaki also used traps to snare smaller game such as raccoon, rabbit, quail, and turkeys. Boys learned to hunt by chasing down these small animals. The area's many lakes and waterways provided great amounts of fish. The Abenaki built wooden fish traps. They also used spears and nets to catch shad and salmon. Their excellent birchbark canoes helped them add to the catch.

Abenaki Farming

Women tapped maple trees for sap (syrup) in the spring. They also gathered wild plants such as blackberries and wild onions during the warm months. Some Abenaki women kept small farms. They grew beans, squash, and maize (corn). Abenaki farmers ground up unused fish parts for plant food and made farming tools from wood or clamshells. The girls learned how to farm and cook from their mothers.

Wild blueberries were gathered for food throughout New Hampshire.

Wigwams

An Abenaki family and close relatives lived in a cone-shaped house called a wigwam. Builders used the trunks of young trees to create a wigwam frame. They covered the frame in mats made of tree bark and animal skins. They left a hole in the ceiling for smoke from their fires to escape. The inside walls were lined with deerskins or bearskins for added warmth during the winter.

Wigwams could be built and taken down quickly.

Some Abenaki preferred to live in oval-shaped longhouses.

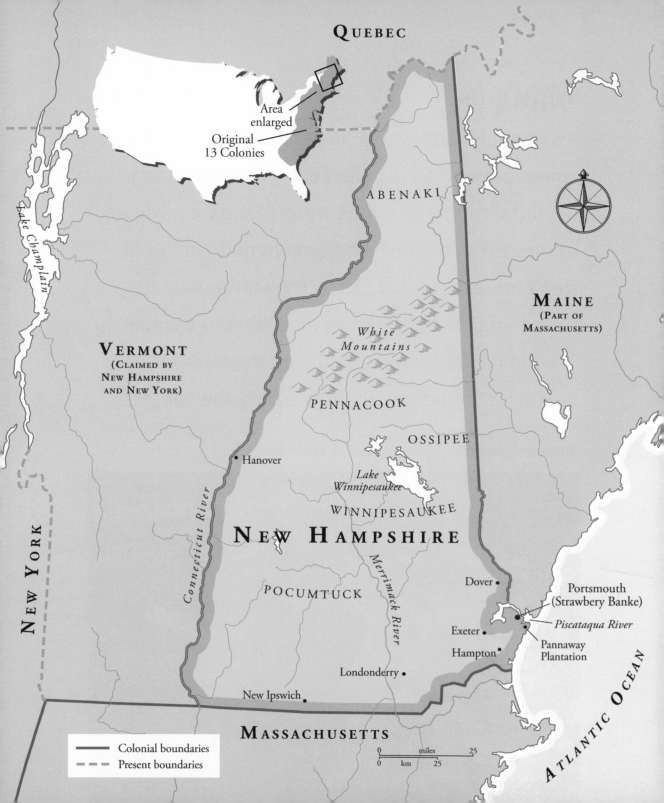

QUEBEC

Area enlarged

Original 13 Colonies

ABENAKI

MAINE
(PART OF
MASSACHUSETTS)

Lake Champlain

VERMONT
(CLAIMED BY
NEW HAMPSHIRE
AND NEW YORK)

White Mountains

PENNACOOK

OSSIPEE

• Hanover

Lake Winnipesaukee

WINNIPESAUKEE

NEW HAMPSHIRE

Connecticut River

Merrimack River

Dover •

Portsmouth
(Strawbery Banke)

Piscataqua River

Exeter •

Pannaway
Plantation

Hampton •

POCUMTUCK

NEW YORK

Londonderry •

New Ipswich •

MASSACHUSETTS

ATLANTIC OCEAN

Colonial boundaries
Present boundaries

miles 25
km 25

CHAPTER 2

The Europeans

Fishing boats from Europe began crossing the Atlantic Ocean to North America in the 1500s. No record exists that any ships explored inside New Hampshire until English trader Martin Pring sailed up the Piscataqua River in 1603. Pring and his men found "goodly groves and woods" on the riverbanks. They did not find the leaves and roots of sassafras trees that Pring hoped to sell as medicine in England.

Though long settled by Native Americans, Europe considered North America a "New World," untouched and without owners.

First Settlements

The king of England gave pharmacist David Thompson a land grant of 6,000 acres (2,400 hectares) on the Piscataqua River in 1623. Thompson and 20 other men constructed a building to live in. They built another structure for trading with the Abenaki. Thompson's farm was named Pannaway Plantation. It soon made money shipping dried fish to England. Pannaway failed after Thompson left. But the towns of Portsmouth and Rye sprang up nearby.

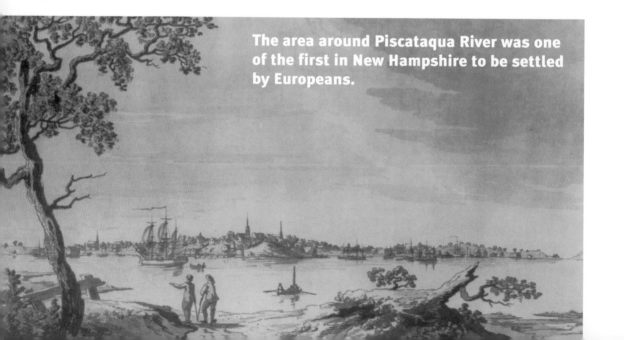

The area around Piscataqua River was one of the first in New Hampshire to be settled by Europeans.

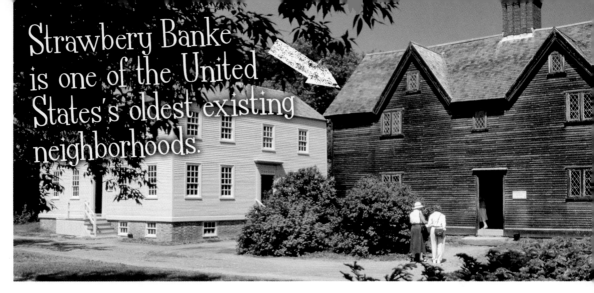

Strawbery Banke is one of the United States's oldest existing neighborhoods.

Today, the Sherburne (left) and Lowd (right) Houses at Strawbery Banke display traditional crafts.

Mason's Colony

Businessman John Mason founded a colony on a land grant located between the Piscataqua and Merrimack Rivers in 1630. Mason was not a settler. He was an **investor**. His first settlement was called Strawbery Banke. It was a business. Mason bought supplies and built houses for colonists. They gave him a share of the money they made selling dried fish. Mason named his colony New Hampshire, after his home county of Hampshire, England.

The Exchange

At first, the Abenaki taught settlers farming, canoe building, and other skills. The English traded guns, glass, and pots and axes made of iron for furs. But the exchange took a tragic turn early on. European diseases such as **smallpox** spread among native peoples starting in 1616. More than 10,000 Abenaki had lived on the land in 1600. The number was down to 1,200 by 1700.

Many native groups around New Hampshire helped settlers when Europeans first arrived.

The Granite State

Granite is a symbol of New Hampshire. People there like to think they share granite's qualities: tough, durable, and not at all flashy. The heavy rock comes from the hardened magma of volcanoes that erupted millions of years ago. Granite is hard but workable. It stands up to all conditions. This makes it perfect for buildings. New Hampshire's granite quarries supplied the stone to build the Library of Congress in Washington, D.C.

The Library of Congress was built with granite mined near Concord, New Hampshire.

Early settlers in
New Hampshire
spent much of
their time clearing
land. They used
the trees they
cut down to build
simple log cabins.

CHAPTER 3

Colony Life

The first years in the wilderness left settlers little time for anything but the struggle to survive. Settlers often had to start making a shelter the day they arrived. New Hampshire's thick forests provided logs for log cabins. Sturdy and warm houses built of brick had become common in major settlements by the 1700s. People living in smaller towns or on the **frontier** continued living in log homes.

Settlers with wives in the old country usually sent for them after a house and property were established.

Working Life

Work filled a colonist's day. Women were responsible for the home. They cooked and cleaned. They also mended clothes and spun wool and flax. Meals sometimes included traditional Abenaki favorites such as succotash (corn and lima beans) and corn bread. Women made soap and candles and tended the gardens next to their houses. Women met together at church or quilting bees. Quilting bees were gatherings where local women sewed blankets while exchanging news.

Colonial women did most of their cooking in or near a large fireplace.

The village blacksmith often was also the dentist.

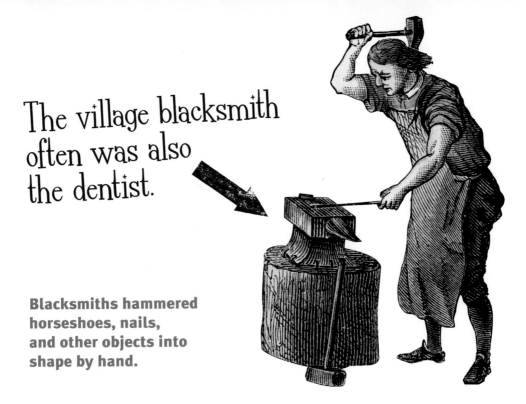

Blacksmiths hammered horseshoes, nails, and other objects into shape by hand.

Both single and married men might work in one of many jobs. The lumber and fishing trades always endured. Farming had become more important in rural areas by the 1700s. Specialties such as blacksmithing and tanning (leather making) provided a good living in towns. Boys wanting to learn a trade served as **apprentices**. Apprentices learned everything necessary to go into business on their own.

In a one-room schoolhouse, students of all ages and levels learned together.

Getting Schooled

The colony's leaders passed a law around 1647 that a town of 50 or more houses had to have a school. Schools usually only had one room. Older students worked at simple tables with the younger students behind them. Everyone sat on wooden planks. The students were closely watched by a male teacher from his desk in the middle of the room.

Girls seldom received an education beyond reading, writing, and a little math. Some boys from wealthy families learned Greek and Latin to prepare for college in England or at Harvard College in Cambridge, Massachusetts. Many children, especially those outside the towns, had only a little education. The boys helped with whatever their fathers did for a living. The girls learned to sew and cook.

Some girls were married as young as 13 or 14.

Girls learned skills at home by helping their mothers.

24

CHAPTER 4

From Colony to Revolution

In 1675 a group of native peoples launched King Philip's War in New England. Fear of raids caused New Hampshire men to set up a **militia**. Trouble between the two sides ramped up as France began to supply Native Americans with weapons. France wanted control of North America. They hoped that backing Native Americans would keep their trade for native furs going while also harming English interests.

Experts estimate 600 settlers and 3,000 Native Americans died in King Philip's War.

Cities throughout the colonies quickly grew during the 1700s.

Growth Spurt

England was now part of Great Britain. It made peace with France in 1713. New settlers soon streamed into the colony of New Hampshire hoping to raise families or make money in trade. People from more expensive colonies such as Massachusetts and Connecticut sought out New Hampshire's cheap land. The biggest group of newcomers was Irishmen of Scottish descent. Their skill growing flax, a source of linen, became a valuable part of New Hampshire's **economy**.

Benning Wentworth was the longest serving colonial governor in any of the colonies. ➤

The Wentworths

Three members of the Wentworth family guided New Hampshire in the 1700s. John Wentworth became lieutenant governor in 1717. That meant that he was second in charge under the **governor**. He served 13 years in office and made peace with the Native Americans. He also encouraged settlers to move into the **interior**. His son Benning made himself rich off the colony as the next governor. New Hampshire grew in size and wealth. The coastal town of Portsmouth became a major New England city.

British redcoats were easily identifiable by their bright red uniform jackets.

The colonies and Great Britain maintained a good relationship into the 1750s, despite complaints about certain British laws or taxes. The colonists continued to share habits and customs with their British cousins. And British help was appreciated in wartime. Conflict came again in 1754. France and its American Indian allies went to war with Britain and its Indian allies again. Colonial militiamen fought alongside British redcoats. The war ended in 1763.

Taxation Without Representation

Great Britain began forcing taxes such as the Sugar Act of 1764 and the Stamp Act of 1765 on the colonists to help pay for the war. The colonists were unhappy that they had no say in the government that created these taxes. Meetings of the New Hampshire Assembly, the colony's elected **legislature**, turned into hours of complaints about the British.

Angry mobs and riots helped convince British officials to get rid of the Stamp Act.

The Problem With Taxes

John Wentworth II was energetic and loyal to the king. He replaced his Uncle Benning in 1767. Wentworth was eager to develop New Hampshire. He ordered roads built to link the colony's towns. But he also faced growing unhappiness. Colonists did not think it fair that Great Britain made laws for them. They wanted a say in how they were governed.

John Wentworth II went on to become royal governor of Nova Scotia.

Representatives argued for a month before deciding on a list of complaints for King George III.

Soon the talk turned to **rebellion** against Britain. Wentworth was alarmed. He dissolved the assembly and the even more rebellious group of legislators that replaced it. The colonists then set up a new Provincial Congress. Representatives from all of the American colonies except Georgia met at a Continental Congress in Philadelphia in September 1774. New Hampshirites Nathaniel Folsom and John Sullivan joined colleagues in writing a list of complaints to King George III.

The raid on Fort William and Mary was accomplished without anyone firing a shot.

Fort William and Mary

The colonists turned against Wentworth when he sent New Hampshire carpenters to build houses for British troops. New Hampshire men struck an early blow against Britain. Four hundred raiders took gunpowder, weapons, and other supplies from Fort William and Mary in Portsmouth on December 13, 1774. Wentworth ordered the raiders arrested. But he lacked the soldiers to enforce the order. Some historians consider the Fort William and Mary raid the American colonists' first military act against Britain.

Off to War

On April 19, 1775, New Hampshire patriots rallied after British troops attacked a rebel storehouse in Concord, Massachusetts. More than 2,000 militiamen under Captain John Stark marched for Boston. They wore clothes made at home. They also carried many different kinds of firearms. The gunpowder and many of the weapons came from Fort William and Mary. In June, New Hampshire sent 911 men to the Battle of Bunker Hill outside Boston.

Captain John Stark leads his soldiers into battle.

A colonist speaks against the way Britain treats the colonies.

CHAPTER 5

The Revolutionary War

Anti-British feeling in New Hampshire forced Wentworth to flee in August 1775. He never returned. The Provincial Congress took over. The representatives almost immediately ceased referring to New Hampshire as a colony. Official documents made it clear they considered it an independent state. In January 1776, the legislature created a **constitution** for the state of New Hampshire. The state declared its independence on June 15.

New Hampshire set up a government independent of Great Britain in January 1776.

Captain John Stark

John Stark was the son of a Scotch-Irish father. He survived capture by Native Americans, frontier explorations, and war with France before the American Revolution. He was present at numerous battles. But he became famous as the "Hero of Bennington." His New Hampshire militia helped defeat British-German forces near Bennington, Vermont, in 1777. Stark later sent a letter to Bennington veterans that ended, "Live free or die: Death is not the worst of evils." Live Free or Die became New Hampshire's state motto in 1945.

John Stark had been made a general by the end of the Revolutionary War.

Independence and Onward

On July 4, 1776, the New Hampshire representatives Bartlett, Whipple, and Thornton signed the Declaration of Independence. The declaration detailed why the colonies were breaking from Great Britain. By then battles had already been fought in Massachusetts and the Carolinas. New Hampshire supplied troops to the Continental army throughout the Revolutionary War. New Hampshire men were especially skilled at fighting in the woods. Many also served at sea.

Thomas Jefferson wrote the Declaration of Independence in seventeen days, before delivering it to Congress.

This is one of Jefferson's early drafts of the Declaration of Independence.

Privateers helped protect colonial ports by overtaking British warships.

Facing Threats

An unknown number of New Hampshire militia and sailors died in the war. Not a single battle was fought in New Hampshire during the war. But Portsmouth faced a serious and constant threat from the powerful British navy. Privately owned warships called privateers fought back against British ships. The Portsmouth shipyard also built three warships for the new Continental navy. They were named *Raleigh*, *America*, and *Ranger*.

Portsmouth merchants suffered during the war, but surrounding farmers fared better.

Close to 95,000 people lived in New Hampshire when the British surrendered on October 19, 1781. The state faced a nearly ruined economy. British warships had destroyed trade by bottling up Portsmouth merchant ships. New Hampshire had also borrowed money to pay for the war. The farmers had done well, though. Their crops fed the Continental army. But they sometimes had trouble getting paid by the Continental government.

New Hampshire's Founding Fathers

Many colonists were unhappy with the British government by early 1776. Parliament had forced many new laws on the colonists without giving them any say in the matter. The Continental Congress agreed to declare independence after months of debate. Congress members John Adams, Benjamin Franklin, Thomas Jefferson, Robert R. Livingston, and Roger Sherman delivered a copy of a declaration of independence to Congress on June 28. Three members from New Hampshire signed the final declaration on July 4.

Josiah Bartlett

Physician Josiah Bartlett had worked on the frontier in Kingston, New Hampshire, before going into politics. He served in three Continental Congresses. He later became chief justice of the New Hampshire Supreme Court. He was chosen to be a U.S. senator but declined the post and instead became state governor.

William Whipple

Whipple was born in Maine. He became a Portsmouth merchant and later was elected to the Second Continental Congress. He led New Hampshire's militia in the battles of Stillwater, Saratoga, and Rhode Island.

Matthew Thornton

Thornton came to the colonies from Ireland at age three and later became a physician. He had only been a member of the Continental Congress seven months when he signed the declaration.

The Ninth State

The peace treaty with Britain was signed in September 1783. But it soon became clear that the new country needed a permanent constitution. Representatives met in 1787 to create one. They then sent it to each former colony to vote on. Representatives from across New Hampshire gathered in the town of Exeter during the summer of 1788 to discuss the matter. New Hampshire voted to adopt the U.S. Constitution on June 21 and became the ninth state of the United States. ★

Portsmouth continued to grow and prosper after statehood.

True Statistics

Number of Abenaki in 1600: More than 10,000

Number of Abenaki in 1700: 1,200

Number of New Hampshire founders who signed the Declaration of Independence: 3

Number of Wentworths who led the colony: 3

Number of New Hampshire soldiers at Bunker Hill: 911

Number of Revolutionary War battles fought in New Hampshire: 0

Number of people in New Hampshire after the revolution: 95,000

Number of states that signed the U.S. Constitution before New Hampshire: 8

Did you find the truth?

(F) New Hampshire Colony was begun by people wanting freedom to practice their religion.

(T) The Stamp Act was very unpopular.

Resources

Books

Deady, Kathleen. *The New Hampshire Colony*. Mankato, MN: Capstone, 2006.

Hazen, Walter A. *Everyday Life: Colonial Times*. Culver City, CA: Good Year, 2008.

Heinrichs, Ann. *New Hampshire*. Mankato, MN: Compass Point, 2004.

Mis, Melody S. *The Colony of New Hampshire*. New York: PowerKids Press, 2006.

Ryan, Marla Felkins, and Linda Schmittroth. *Tribes of Native America: Abenaki*. San Diego: Blackbirch, 2003.

Shannon, Terry M. *New Hampshire*. New York: Children's Press, 2009.

Thomas, William D. *New Hampshire*. New York: Gareth Stevens, 2007.

Organizations and Web Sites

Abenaki Nation: St. Francis/Sokoki Band

www.abenakination.org
Learn about Abenaki history and find out what's going on today on an Abenaki reservation in Vermont.

New Hampshire Historical Society—Museum

www.nhhistory.org/museum.html
Study exhibits offering details on the history and culture of New Hampshire's people.

Places to Visit

American Independence Museum

One Governors Lane
Exeter, NH 03833
(603) 772-2622
www.independencemuseum.org
Learn about how an Exeter family lived at the time of the American Revolution.

Strawbery Banke Museum

14 Hancock Street
Portsmouth NH, 03801
(603) 433-1100
www.strawberybanke.org
Explore historic houses and work with hands-on exhibits to see how people have lived in New Hampshire for the last 400 years.

Important Words

apprentices (uh-PREN-tis-ez) —people who learn a skill by working with an expert

constitution (kahn-sti-TOO-shun)—the laws of a country or state that specify the rights of the people and the powers of that government

economy (ih-KA-nuh-mee)—the system of buying, selling, and making things and managing money

frontier (fruhn-TEER)—the far edge of settled territory or country

governor (GUHV-uh-nhur)—a person who controls or exercises authority over an area

interior (in-TEER-ee-ur)—a remote area away from the shore

investor (in-VEST-uhr)—a person who gives or lends money with the intention of getting more back

legislature (LEJ-is-lay-chur)—a group of people who have the power to make or change laws

militia (muh-LISH-uh)—a group of people who are trained to fight but who aren't professional soldiers

rebellion (ri-BEL-yuhn)—an open opposition to a ruling authority

smallpox (SMAWL-pahks)—a contagious disease that causes a rash, high fever, and blisters

Index

Page numbers in **bold** indicate illustrations

About the Author

Kevin Cunningham has written more than 40 books on disasters, the history of disease, Native Americans, and other topics. Cunningham lives near Chicago with his wife and young daughter.